# Navigating the world of digital social communication

A guidebook for people with autism and their families

Autism West Midlands • UK

Navigating the world of digital social communication - A guidebook for people with autism and their families



Published by Autism West Midlands



ISBN-13: 978-0-9576541-7-4

# Contents

# Introduction

The Internet is a combination of networks that almost all computers are connected to. Devices such as smartphones (iPhones, android phones etc.) and tablets (iPads, android tablets etc.) can also link into the network, as can other smart items such as televisions. Technology is constantly progressing and the Internet is linking up more and more things. This is great for you because it means you have access to more and more of the world's knowledge and information as well as the opportunity to meet and interact with new people and old friends, no matter where they are in the world.

Being able to use new technology is an important part of life for most teenagers and adults. You can use the Internet for activities like banking, buying tickets to events, ordering food, DVDs and clothes, as well as socialising with your friends and family. Social networking and text messaging allow you to talk to people who live far away, and they can be useful if you don't want to speak to somebody face-to-face.

Many people on the spectrum find it easier to communicate through typing rather than speech, so social networking can also be a more comfortable way for you to socialise with others. As well as this, talking online and by text means there are no facial expressions, no body language, and no sensory problems to deal with. You can also pause and think before you write something, so you have more time and space to say exactly what you want. By bringing together large numbers of people, social networks are also great places to discuss shared interests. Whichever site you use, it is likely that you will be able to find a group or forum especially for your interests. It is therefore extremely important that you know how to behave safely and appropriately when online and when using a mobile phone.

## Why is behaving appropriately online important?

As mobile phones and social networks make it easier for you to speak to more people, it is also important that you do not offend others or make them feel uncomfortable. A lot of socialising is now done online, so many of your friends will get an idea of you based on what you say and do on the Internet. Many people, including your friends and family, will not expect you to behave differently online compared to how you behave in person. Behaving appropriately – for example, knowing when and how often to talk to someone – will help to make sure that you are not upsetting others online.

Things that you upload onto the Internet will stay there forever. Once you've sent or uploaded a message or a photograph there is no way of getting it back. There is no way of knowing where the things that you post on the Internet or send to somebody's mobile phone will end up. Even pictures that you send to your friends may end up online, where other people will be able to see them.

There are lots of ways that people can take those things and put them online, including taking screenshots. They might do this for a number of reasons.

**Screenshots**

Screenshots are pictures taken of the screen of whatever device they are using, and whatever is displayed at that time. This can be done in various ways depending on the device and creates an image file that can be sent to other people.

The person that you send the photo to may decide to put it onto the internet because they think it would be funny for other people see it. Some people may not be very good friends, so they might want to put the photo onto the Internet to embarrass you. Your friends may not know if you want your photo to be shared with other people or not. Be completely sure that you know what a friend is and who your friends are.

If you are sending something to a friend then make sure that they know that the photo is just for them, and that you do not want it to be put onto the Internet or shown to other people. But if it is a photo or a message that you are not comfortable sharing with people that you do not know, then it is much safer not to send it to anybody.

## What is a friend?

Friendship can be hard to understand and the rules can be complicated. This is even truer with real life friends, online friends and "Facebook friends". Each of these three types of friend is very different and the rules vary between them. Real life friends are friends that you know in real life. So this means your friends from school, college, university or work; or from social and leisure activities that you do. These friends are the people you meet to go to the cinema or to their house to play video games. These friends are the safest kind of friend because you know who they are and what their motivations are. If you know someone in this way but you are not quite friends with them, because you haven't known them long enough or got to know them well enough, then they are acquaintances. When you are online you may add your real life friends and acquaintances as friends on social media sites and talk to them in forums or in games.

You can also add and speak to people you have only met online. They may share your interests or play the same game as you and you may have met them through that. You may also know them because you have a mutual friend who introduced you online. You could meet an online friend in real life but you should not consider them a true real life friend until you get to know them well.

Finally, "Facebook friends" only means the friends that people have on Facebook. Sometimes complete strangers may send you a friend request, but this does not make them a friend. The profiles can be fake and send out friend requests to pretend to know more people, or they can be profiles for nasty strangers who want to find vulnerable people online. If someone is a Facebook friend but not an online friend or real life friend then they are not a friend at all and you should not talk to them about personal things.

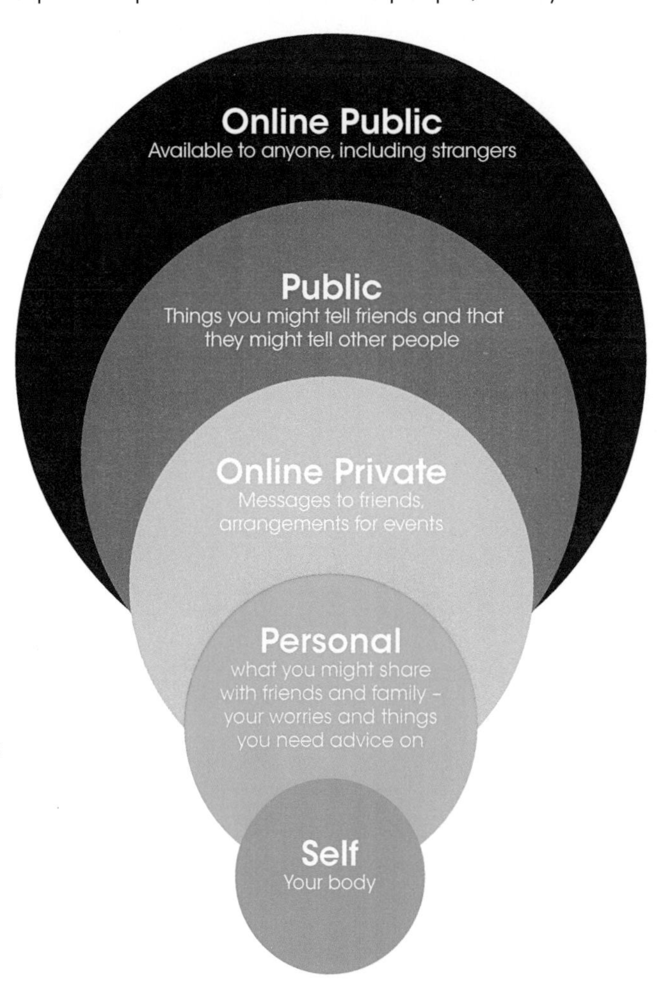


You should talk about different things with different sets of friends. Your close real life friends and your family are the people that you can discuss your problems with and personal things about your life. These people should keep this information private. However, if you write those things online then there is a chance that it will not stay private, so it is better to talk about these things in person or on the phone.

You can use the "private" functions on social media and other websites to discuss basic messages to friends, plans for events and meet-ups and to discuss tactics within a game. These are things that you only want to discuss with friends but, if they were accidentally shown to other people, it would not matter or be embarrassing.

In real life, public information is information that other people might know about you, such as your favourite band. This is not a secret and it would not be embarrassing for others to find out about it. However, "public" means something different online. It means that anyone at all can see information about you. And so total strangers can find out your favourite band and your favourite film, if you have posted this online, as can potential employers and your parents. More importantly, people can also see the messages, photos and updates you have added. This means you should be very careful what you post online and be aware that it is visible to anyone in the world.

## Using the Internet in everyday life

The Internet is an incredibly valuable resource. You can use it to talk to friends, learn new things and follow the latest news and trends, as well as buying shopping and services and banking online. It is important to understand all of the tools available to you as well as the potential risks and how to keep yourself safe. You can download programmes and 'apps' to help you with all of your day-to-day tasks and activities as well as ones to support you with your difficulties and anxieties. You can research online using Google to find things that might help you as well as fun games and tools that will brighten your day!

## Google

Google is an online search tool, sometimes called a search engine. If you visit www.google.com, you can type anything into the search bar and find a huge range of results. This will help you to find events and services in your area as well as details about places you might visit, to help you to prepare. You can also search for tools and apps that might help you and websites about your favourite things. Through these searches you may be able to find a group or message board about your particular interests and be able to meet other people who like the same things. There are other search tools, including Bing or Ask, but Google is the most popular.

## Apps

"Apps" is used as a shortened version of the word 'applications'. They can be used on smartphones and some kinds of computers, notably those running Windows 8. Apps can be specially designed versions of websites that have simplified the functions of the website to make an easier, more efficient version to use on a phone or tablet. They can also be totally self-contained apps that offer a particular service, function or game. There are thousands of different apps and you can find them in the app store if you have an iPhone or iPad, the play store if you have an android phone or tablet and the windows store if you have a windows phone or tablet, or a PC running windows 8. Some apps are free and others cost money. All of the providers require you to sign up for an account and the play and app stores also require credit or debit card details at sign up. You have to do this even if you only want to download free apps. There are also things you can buy within the game called 'in-app purchases'. These are often items or levels in games. So even free games and apps may ask for you to pay to continue to play or to improve your playing experience. Remember, these are purchases exactly like you would make in a real shop, they cost real money and can add up over time to be extremely expensive. Be very careful what you buy within games. And if it is not your credit or debit card then do not purchase anything without permission from whoever owns the card.

**Angry Birds**

This is a game in which players use a slingshot to fire a bird at a structure containing pigs. The aim is to destroy all of the pigs. This is one of the biggest apps and is an incredibly popular game.

**Bejewelled Blitz**

This is a very popular game in which you match rows of 'jewels' that look the same and then they disappear. The aim is to collect points and gain special gems.

**Candy Crush**

Another very popular game that asks players to match items that look the same, this time 'sweets'. The aim is to move to higher levels and more difficult puzzles.

## Web Browsers

A web browser is the tool you use to view web pages on the Internet. You can download all the different browsers available. Most devices come with a browser already installed but you can download most other browsers to get the one you prefer. Apple devices come with Safari and cannot run Internet Explorer, Android devices come with Chrome and cannot run Safari and Windows devices come with Internet Explorer and cannot run Safari.

## Email

Most email providers have an app that you can use to check your email in a more convenient and streamlined way, rather than using the mobile site.

## Internet Banking

Banking online is a great way to get your banking done quickly and efficiently. You can check your balance, make payments to people and pay bills, without going into a bank branch or even leaving your house. You can do this on the bank's website or using their app. You will need to register for Internet banking, with your bank, before you can begin. Different banks have different systems and a variety of security systems so you will have to visit the bank's website to learn more about how to use their services. Mobile and Internet banking can carry more risks than banking in a branch because you need to use passwords and people may be able to steal these. This means you should be extremely careful about where you do your banking, ensuring other people can't see your password and you shouldn't share the password with anyone else. If you have any concerns about your banking and security, you should contact your bank immediately.

## Online Shopping

Shopping online can be a great way to shop quickly and conveniently and avoid the sometimes-stressful experience of visiting shops. It means you can take your time and search all over the world for the items you want. There are lots of different online shops and websites that act like a marketplace allowing different people to sell their items. eBay is a particularly famous example of an online shopping site and you can find a huge variety of items on there. It is important to remember that while shopping online may be great for many items, if you find some textures itchy or have sensory issues, it may still be better to try clothes on in a shop before you buy them.

Shopping online requires a credit or debit card, or a PayPal account linked to a credit or debit card. This is how you pay for the items. It is important to remember that shopping online is just like shopping in a shop because you have to use real money to buy the items and so you should be sure you can afford the items you agree to pay for.

Shopping online can make you more vulnerable to having your account stolen and so you should be careful to keep your passwords safe and, if you think there is a problem or you are worried someone has been using your account then you must contact your bank immediately.

### eBay

eBay is a website where people can add items to sell and buy items added by other people. As a seller you can also set up a store, which is like a webpage and shows all of your items in one place, allowing people to browse. Some people use it to run their retail business and others use it to sell personal items that they no longer need. Some items are in auctions and you have to bid for them and try to outbid other people. Other items have a "Buy it Now" option and you can just purchase the item at the price stated.

You can search for items you like, buy them and then rate and review your purchases. People with a high percentage of top-level ratings have been good sellers in the past and so you should try to buy off these people. Sometimes people sell items that don't exist or take money without sending the item. This is rare but you should check the seller's ratings and reviews before buying from them, as this will help you to know you can trust them.

### PayPal

PayPal is an online service that allows you to create an account and link it to a credit or debit card. This means you can pay for things on websites without entering your card details, making your purchases safer and quicker. Other people can also make payments to you through PayPal, which prevents you having to give out personal information such as bank details, to receive payments.

## Social Media

Social media is the term used to describe sites that offer the chance to communicate information in a social way, allowing users to interact with news and current affairs. This is different to news sites, which deliver news and information but do not allow users to engage directly with the story. Social Media is generally understood to include Facebook, Twitter and YouTube but also includes lots of other sites that offer similar services.

These sites allow you to upload images, post links and write your own status updates or 'tweets' and some also allow you to directly contribute to news and information articles. You can use this to write about yourself and your life, or to comment on things that you think are important. But remember, the Internet is there forever and you should not post anything offensive or that might embarrass you or anyone else. The law still applies online so you should also be careful not to post anything illegal such as untrue things about other people that make them look bad or claims about them that are not true – these are called defamation of character and libel and are both illegal. You should also be careful not to comment in a way that may make someone feel uncomfortable.

## Selfies

"Selfies" are pictures you take of yourself usually using a smartphone or tablet. Lots of people take these and post them on social networking sites.

Most people post selfies where they think they look particularly attractive but some are pictures of the person in a particular place or with a particular person. Posting selfies is usually seen by other people to be showing off and sometimes this is ok but people generally don't like when others post too many selfies as they think this comes across as attention seeking. Some people feel that taking the picture from an angle slightly higher than your face makes you look more attractive. This is sometimes called a "MySpace" pose. Other people take the photos of their reflection in a mirror. Or you could take a selfie with another person.

Sometimes people will make comments about the picture and these won't always be nice but you should just ignore any negative comments but consider not posting another selfie or blocking that person from seeing your profile. Equally, you should not post nasty comments on other people's selfie pictures or tell them that you think they are attention seeking.

## Over sharing

It is possible to share too much when communicating with others, be that in person or online. Sometimes people will say you have given them 'too much information' which is when they think you have shared something unpleasant that they would rather not know, such as information about bodily functions or sexual encounters. It is best to avoid talking too much about these things because they may make people uncomfortable. You may occasionally talk in more detail about these things with certain types of people, such as discussing bodily functions with your doctor if you are unwell, or talking about romantic partners with close friends. However, you should never write about these things online. This is because the information will be there forever and may embarrass you in the future. It is also likely to make others unhappy and uncomfortable.

Another kind of over sharing is telling people lots of things that they are not interested in. It is ok to add pictures and comments about your life and the things you like but you should pick out the interesting details that other people might want to know about. For example, you should not post about things that are very common and that lots of other people might have done, such as eating a sandwich. You should instead post about the more important events in your life - like if you have made a great achievement at work or have a funny story about your day - and things that might interest your online friends - like if you have a night out planned with a group of friends, you might tag them in a status to say you are looking forward to it. If you are adding a comment to something involving other people, such as a comment on a status update or in a forum conversation, then you should be careful to check that you are adding something to the conversation and keeping to the topic being discussed.

People often post selfies, pictures of things they like and pictures of food, particularly using Instagram. However, you should limit the number of times you do this. Posting lots of pictures that look the same is very boring and annoying for other people. If you want to take pictures of your food, you should limit it to meals that were particularly special or delicious, rather than taking photos of all of your ordinary meals.

**Sharing**

A picture of an attractive meal in a fancy restaurant

Talking about having been ill but feeling better

Talking about the time you visited the science museum in a conversation about science museums

**Over sharing**

A photo of a ham sandwich and a glass of water

Talking about how much snot you had to clear up while you were ill

Talking about the time you visited the science museum in a conversation about hairstyles or football

# When to comment on someone else's post

If someone posts a picture of himself or herself, it is OK to say they look nice but only if you know them well. If they are of the opposite sex then they may think you are sexually attracted to them and so you should be careful to only comment if you are friends with that person. It is also a good idea not to be the only person to comment on a picture of somebody of the opposite sex, as it can look overly keen. If you are not heterosexual and the other person knows this and they are of the same gender, then they may also think you find them sexually attractive. Again, you should not be overly keen and you should only comment if you know the person well. It is never OK to tell a person that they do not look nice in their picture.

If somebody posts a picture of his or her child or family then it is OK to say something nice about the photo or say that the child is cute but you should only ever do this if you know the person well.

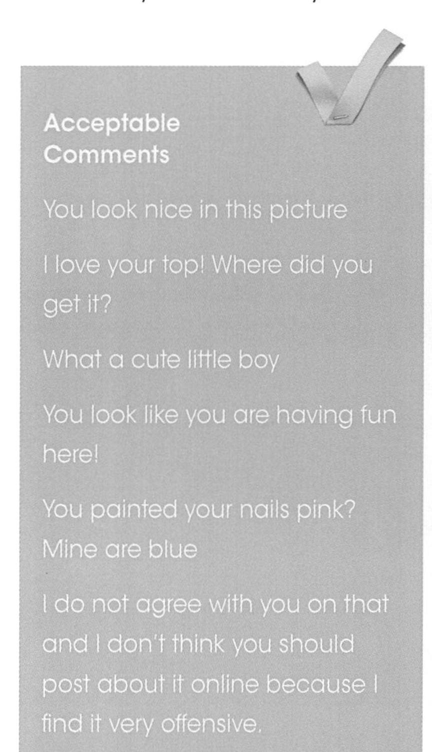


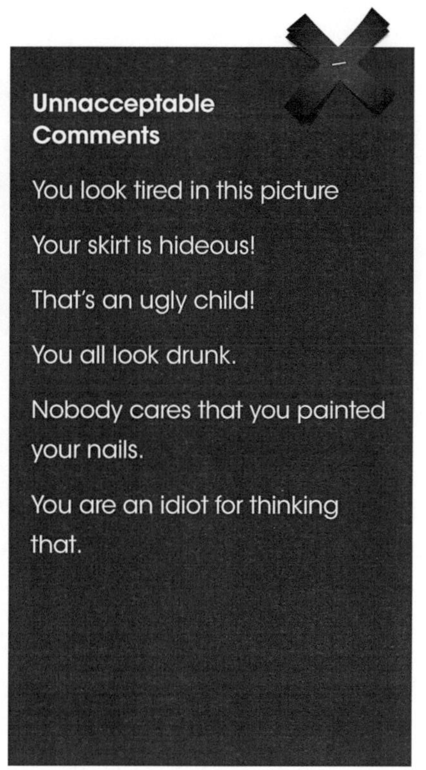


Commenting on family photos of people you don't know may make people quite uncomfortable. It is never OK to say something about another person's family that is not nice.

If somebody posts a picture or comment about themselves or their life and you have something that you think is relevant to that, then it is OK to comment. Again, it is important that you know the person so that you commenting on their life does not make them feel uncomfortable. If you think that what they have said is boring or stupid, you do not need to tell them this. However, if you think what they have said is very offensive then you might comment to say that, but you should give a very short description of what you find offensive rather than calling them names. It is not ok to criticise poor spelling, punctuation and grammar, even if you find this offensive.

The flowchart on the next page can help you decide whether or not to post a comment.

Should I comment?
Do you know the person?
Yes
No
What kind of website are you on?
What kind of website are you on?
Social network
Forum or message board
Forum or message board
Social Media
What kind of post is it that you want to comment on?
What kind of post is it that you want to comment on?
Do you have something useful to contribute to the conversation?
Do not comment
picture of
e person or
eir family/
ends
A comment or update
Public or asking for comments
Private or marked as no comments
Do not comment
Yes
Add your comment
How well do you know them?
How well do you know them?
Not at all
Do not comment
No
Do not comment
very
or not
ll
Friend or family
Friend, family or acquaintance
Do you want to say something nice or a reasonable objection to the post?
Do not comment
Do you want to say something nice or a reasonable objection to the post?
No
Yes
Do not comment
Add your comment
Do you want to say something nice?
No
Yes
Do not comment
Add your comment
Yes
No
Do not comment
Add your comment

### Facebook

Facebook is one of the world's largest social networking sites and also has an app. People use it to share photos and videos as well as post updates about their lives. Most people post things about something interesting that they have done, for example a holiday that they have been on or an event that they have been to. The site is a useful tool for communicating with people all over the world. Most people only add people they know in real life, either as a friend or as an acquaintance, so that they can learn more about that person. If somebody adds you and you don't know him or her, sometimes they might be a friend of a friend who wants to say hello. If this is the case, then they should send you a message before adding you or ask the shared friend to tell you to add them. If this does not happen then you should not add them because they are a stranger. If you just don't want to add someone as a friend then you don't have to.

On Facebook, you can select who gets to see your status updates, photos, and other stuff. You can do this using the 'audience selector' tool. You can use this to make sure that only your friends and family see your updates. Only people who are your friends can post messages on your timeline. You can 'unfriend' someone if you don't want him or her to post on your timeline. You can also 'block' people. 'Blocking' somebody stops him or her from starting conversations with you or viewing things that you post on your Timeline. People will not be told if you have blocked them.

## Twitter

Twitter is a 'micro blogging' site. This means that users post their thoughts, beliefs and opinions as well as sharing links, images and videos, but they do so in 140 characters or less. This is called a Tweet. Lots of large companies, businesses and organisations also have Twitter pages where they share news and information.

When you sign up to Twitter, you can decide whether to make your Tweets public or private. Public is the default setting. It means that your Tweets are visible to anyone, whether they have a Twitter account or not. Protected Tweets are only visible to your approved Twitter followers. People will have to request to follow you. This allows you to control who can view your Tweets. To protect your Tweets, you will have to go to your 'Security and privacy settings', scroll down to the 'Tweet privacy' section and tick the box next to 'Protect my Tweets'. You then need to click 'Save' at the bottom of the page. If you change your mind about who you want to be able to see your Tweets, you can change these settings at any time.

You can also block people on Twitter. To do this, simply go to the person's profile page, click the gear icon, and select 'Block'. This means that the person will no longer be able to follow you, so you can control who can see your information.

Other people can see what you post on Twitter and there have been cases recently where people have been arrested for tweets that they posted. The law still applies on Twitter so do not post anything that is offensive or illegal.

### YouTube

YouTube is a video sharing website. Users can add, share and comment on videos about almost anything but there are some filters and a report function to prevent videos that are criminal, graphic or sexually explicit. Users can also create their own page to add their videos to. YouTube in particular is known for very negative comments on videos and so you should be careful what you post and ignore rude remarks. If comments are causing you concern or distress, you can hide all comments or report them. If you are still worried, talk to a trusted relative about it.

Be very careful before uploading anything that may be copyrighted (created by someone other than you). This includes images, video, clips of gameplay or music. If you haven't created the content yourself then you should not upload it. YouTube may ban users who upload content they haven't created themselves.

### Wikipedia

Wikipedia is an online encyclopaedia that has pages about all different things, added by anyone and edited and moderated by a team of volunteer editors. Each page is called a 'wiki' and you can find them about lots of things but, because the general public adds them, they are not always accurate. They may also be wrong because people have added them or changed them as a joke or are biased in some way. Wikipedia has lots of great information and is a great starting point for further research, but don't believe something just because you saw it on Wikipedia.

## Instagram

Instagram is an app that allows users to take pictures and add special filters to them to make them look more stylised. You then post them to your 'feed', which is a list of all of the pictures you have taken. You can also 'follow' other people which means you can see the photos they post. Instagram is often used for selfies and pictures of food.

By default, any photos that you upload to Instagram are public and can be viewed by anyone. If you only want your followers to see your photos, then you need to set you profile to private by setting the 'Photos are private' switch at the bottom of your profile page to 'ON'. When your profile is set to private, people who want to see your photos will have to send you a follow request, which you can then either accept or deny. This allows you to control who sees your photos but you should only post pictures you are happy to share with your friends, as Instagram is not a secure way to share personal pictures or information.

On Instagram, it is also possible to add your photos to a 'Photo Map', which means that people can see where a picture was taken. You may not want people to see where you took your photos, especially if they were taken at your home. Like on other social networks, Instagram allows you to block other users from seeing your account. You can also report users, photos, and comments that you think are inappropriate. Remember; do not post any photos that you are not comfortable with. People may ask you to upload photos of yourself that are inappropriate. If this happens, do not upload any photos and tell a trusted relative immediately.

**Tumblr.**

Tumblr. is a website where you can post different pictures, videos and blog posts to build a page that represents your personality. This is used to then engage with other people and discuss your shared interests and things that you like. However, a lot of people use the site to post adult content, which means it is sexually explicit. If you see this sort of content and it makes you uncomfortable then you should leave the blog or page that you are on and avoid it in future.

# Hashtags #

The # symbol is used to mark keywords or topics in a post. It is used a lot on Instagram and Twitter. People use the hashtag symbol # before a relevant keyword or phrase (no spaces) in their post to categorise them and help them show more easily in searches. Hashtags can occur anywhere in the post – at the beginning, middle, or end. Hashtagged words that become very popular sometimes become Trending Topics on Twitter. This means that lots of people are talking about them at the same time. Sometimes people use hashtags to say how they're feeling or indicate the tone of the post, for example #badday or #sarcasm.

# Poking

Poking is a function on Facebook that allows you to click a button and the other person gets a notification saying they have been poked. This is meant to be a bit silly and just fun for friends. Some people also use it to suggest that they are romantically interested in someone else. If a friend pokes you, it is normal to poke them back once you see the notification that they have poked you. If someone you don't know pokes you, it is best to ignore him or her. The flowchart on the next page can help you decide whether or not to poke someone.

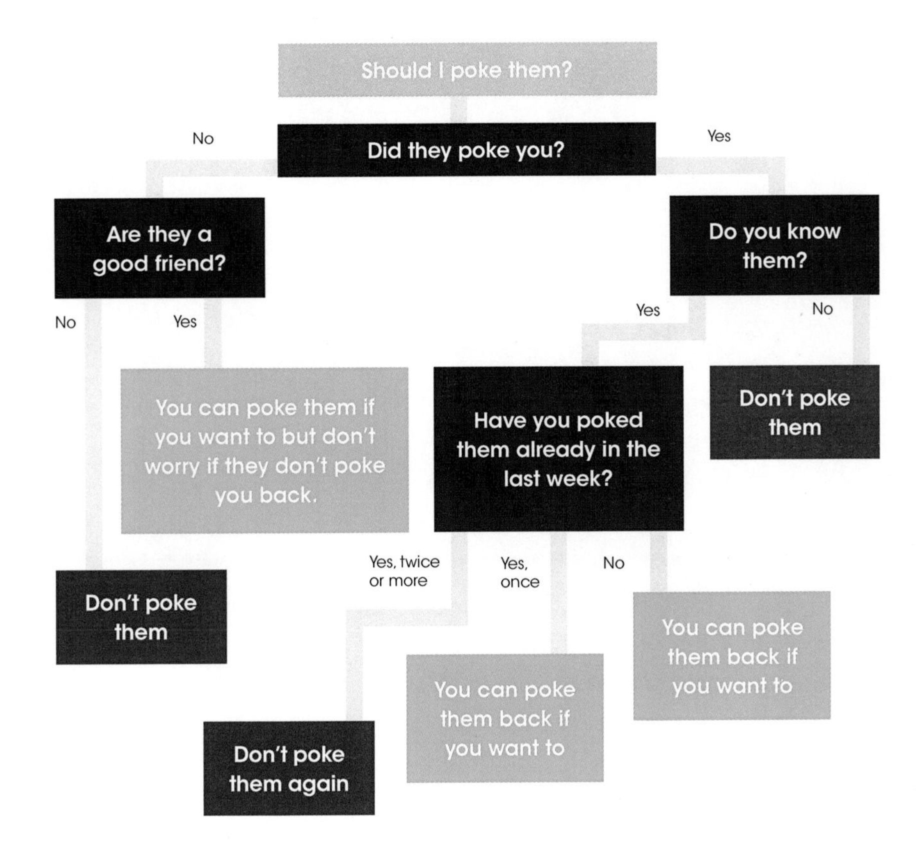
Should I poke them?
Did they poke you?
No
Yes
Are they a good friend?
Do you know them?
No
Yes
Yes
No
You can poke them if you want to but don't worry if they don't poke you back.
Have you poked them already in the last week?
Don't poke them
Yes, twice or more
Yes, once
No
Don't poke them
You can poke them back if you want to
You can poke them back if you want to
Don't poke them again

# Reputation and the way you speak

Your reputation is what other people think about you. It is important for you to have a good reputation if you want to meet new people, get along with others and do well in life, gaining employment and experiences. In real life, we manage our reputation by being kind to people, gaining a good education and getting involved in things that will give us good experience in different areas. To be successful in gaining a good reputation, we have to do good things and have that recognised by other people. This means that communication with others is vital for a good reputation. This does not mean that we have to get along with everyone we meet but it does suggest that we should be polite and considerate, even to those people we don't like, to ensure that the people that matter to us can see that we are good people.

Managing your reputation is just as important online as it is in real life. You need to be aware of the way you talk to others and communicate ideas and ensure that this is appropriate and reflects your personality in a good way. Things that are online stay online and are there for all to see. This means you should be careful to only post things that won't upset or offend others and you should not post things when you are angry or upset because you may say things that make you look bad because you are not thinking clearly.

The world is becoming more and more aware of the Internet and the information available on it. This means that employers and other people, including new friends and romantic interests, are likely to look you up online. You must be sure that they will only find things that show you in a good way and make you seem like a good person. This means that you should not post lots of pictures of yourself drinking or doing anything illegal. It also means that you should not post any pictures that have a sexual element to them, or write offensive or inappropriate things. Other people, including people you didn't want to show them to, could see these and this can make them judge you badly. There are lots of ways to change your privacy settings to make it more difficult for employers to see these things, but you should not rely on these entirely. It is more important to make sure that your profiles and accounts are appropriate.

**LinkedIn**

LinkedIn is a website for professionals that allows you to add a small profile and all of your previous experience and job roles. You can also add skills and interests and other people can endorse you to show that they think you have those skills. Employers are very likely to look for you on this site if you apply for a job so it is a good place to write down all of your experience and it is vital that you keep this profile highly professional.

## "Tone"

The tone of a message means the way that it sounds or comes across to the other person. Just like when you are speaking, your words can seem different depending on how you say them. If you are very excited and happy then you may speak more loudly or quickly and with lots of body movements to show your excitement. If you are quite sad then you may talk more quietly or slowly. You may also use different language and tone when you talk to different people. With your family and friends you might be more open about how you are feeling and express your emotions quite clearly. You might also use informal language, jokes and slang. However, when you are talking to someone more official like an employer or a teacher, you may use more formal language and be more careful not to let your emotions affect the way you speak. This is because you want to make a polite and respectful impression on these people, to show that you take their opinions and position seriously. However, when you are with friends, you are an equal and can express yourself as fully as you want to. It is important, though, that you do not point out if you think somebody else is using poor grammar, punctuation and spelling, or if you think that they have used the wrong tone – this can be seen as rude and can make the other person feel embarrassed.

Sometimes you may feel angry and this may affect the way you talk and communicate. Generally though it is better to try to not let your communication be affected by anger. If you are feeling angry you should walk away from the situation – be that a person, your computer or your phone or tablet – and take a break from it. Once you have had time to calm down, you will be able to think more clearly about the situation; what made you angry? What would make you feel better? If you think you need to continue your conversation with the other person or people then you should speak to them calmly and clearly and explain your point of view and what you disagree with about what they said or did. However, if the thing that made you angry is beyond your control – such as your train was late or something you were working on went wrong – then you should just try to remain calm and not let the anger and worry affect the way you talk to others. Equally, if somebody being unnecessarily cruel or unkind has upset you, it is often best to ignore it because they usually say these things to get a response from you and so getting angry is giving them what they want.

It is important to get the tone right for your communications and there are different rules for different kind of communication. Letters and CVs have a very formal structure that you can easily research and learn and you should use formal language. Formal language is the sort of language used in official documents and it usually means avoiding contracted words (such as "don't" or "can't"). If you read a letter out loud, it should not sound like how you talk normally. Do not swear or use any slang words and ensure that you use proper spelling, grammar and punctuation. Exclamation marks should only be used if absolutely necessary as they are not considered to be very formal and should never be used on a CV because you may not be taken seriously. Do not use emoticons.

Emails that you send at work or to possible future employers or companies and businesses, should also have a formal tone. You should again avoid slang and simple language that you might use when you are talking. You should be clear and precise in delivering your message and, again, be careful to use proper spelling, punctuation and grammar. Do not use emoticons unless you have received a message from the same person before and they used an emoticon.

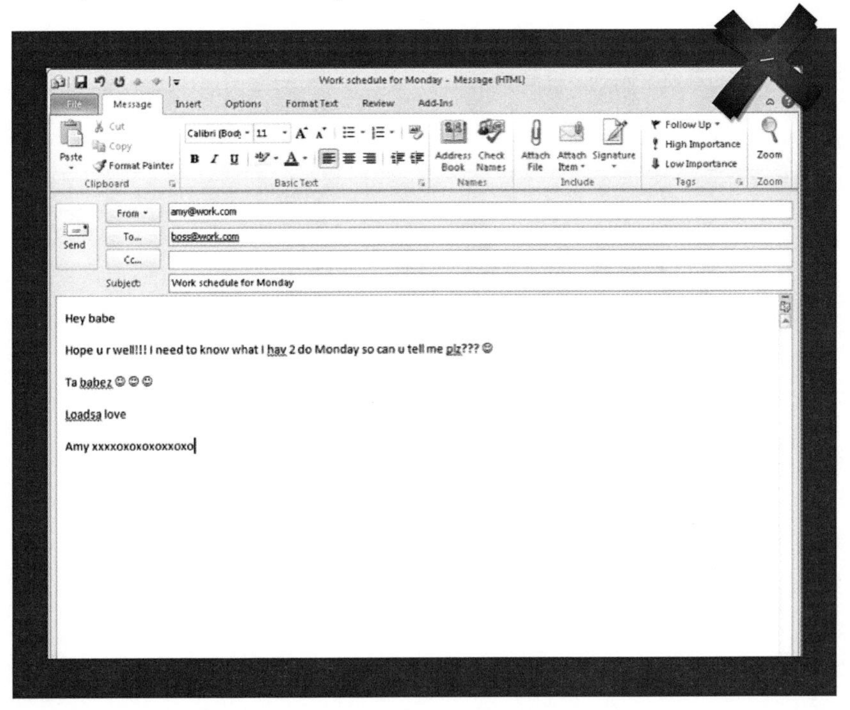

Informal writing is what you should use when talking to friends or other young people you know. You can use slang words and abbreviations – like "lol", "omg" and "wtf" – and your grammar, punctuation and spelling do not matter as much. You should try to write these messages as if you are speaking so they come across as friendly and engaging.

Punctuation and emoticons can also be used more freely in these messages to express your emotions and help the other person to understand what you mean by your messages.

For example, you may use an emoticon to make a reply seem less abrupt or harsh:

**Question: Would you like to come to the cinema with me tonight?**

**Reply 1: No I can't sorry.**

This comes across as a very serious response and may seem to be angry or mean.

**Reply 2: No, I can't sorry** ☹

The sad face makes it clear that you are sad you can't go and makes the reply seem friendlier.

## Mirroring

Mirroring is a very useful technique. It comes from the idea that you act like a reflection in a mirror to behave in the same way as the person you are talking to. You don't have to be physically in front of the other person and it is not the same as copying, where you do the exact same things as that person. Instead, mirroring means that you follow another person's lead on the best tone to use. So, if the person uses exclamation marks, emoticons and slang language, then you can see the tone is informal and you can use these things as well. If they send you a very structured, precise and well-punctuated message, then you should reply in this way. You do not need to start again with this with every conversation – if you have spoken to the same person before then you can use the same style and tone you used last time. If you are very unsure, it is always better to use a formal tone to show respect for the other person and then change to less formal language, if they do.

**Informal**

D'you wanna come to the cinema? :)

How's u?

Okie dokie babe, see u there!

**Formal**

Would you like to come to the cinema with me?

How are you?

That's fine with me, I'll see you there.

## Punctuation

Punctuation can affect the way that your writing comes across. It is designed to show a reader how your words are meant to sound. For example, exclamation marks show that the sentence is very shocking or exciting and question marks show that the sentence is a question. Full stops show that a sentence has ended but in certain contexts they can come across as very harsh or abrupt. If you use a full stop, you are showing that you consider your thoughts the end of the matter and needs no more input from the other person. If the other person expects to have more input or has asked a question then they may be upset that you have ended the conversation. For example:

**Question: Would you like to come to the cinema with me tonight?**

Reply 1: No.

Reply 2: No, I'm sorry I have to help my mum with the dinner tonight.

Both replies use a full stop at the end but the first sentence comes across as quite rude because it ends the sentence with no detail or explanation for the answer. The second one offers a reason for saying no, which shows that you have seriously considered the question and want to give a polite response.

## Emoticons

Emoticons are images that represent facial expressions and emotions. These can be used to communicate with others and show the mood you are in and the way you intend a message to be understood. For example, a smiley face can show someone that you mean what you have said in a friendly way and a sad face can show that you are feeling sad. A face with its tongue sticking out can show that you are joking, because sometimes it is difficult to tell, when the joke is written down, what you meant. Emoticons are made up of different kinds of punctuation but modern chat apps and programmes often automatically convert these to pictures that are included in the programme. Some chat apps also have "stickers" which are pictures based on emoticons but have much more detail and sometimes use cartoon animals or famous characters to show the same things. Here are some examples and their meanings:

| Face | Emotion |
|---|---|
| :-) :) =) =-) | Happy or friendly |
| :D :-D =D =-D | Very happy or excited |
| :( :-( =( =-( | Sad or disappointed |
| :’( :’-( | Very sad and crying |
| ;) ;-) | Flirty or joking depending on context |
| :p :-P =p =-P | Joking or being silly |
| :s =S | Worried, concerned or confused |
| o.O O.o | Confused |
| :/ | Unsure or apathetic |
| >:( | Angry |
| :o =O | Shocked |
| ^_^ | Cute or happy |

**Polite/friendly use of punctuation and emoticons**

No, I can't☹thank you though!

Happy Birthday!☺

Yes, that's fine☺

You're so funny!

**Abrupt/rude use of punctuation**

No I can't thank you though.

Happy Birthday.

Yes that's fine.

You're so funny.

**The difference between the examples above:**

The green example shows that you are sad that you can't go whereas the red implies that you don't care.

The red example is quite abrupt for a celebration; the green example uses an exclamation mark to seem more positive and excited

The red example comes across as if it is not fine and you are a bit annoyed. The green shows that you are happy and genuinely ok with the situation.

The red example seems sarcastic and irritated whereas the green seems happy and excited because the other person is genuinely funny.

# Messaging

You have a range of different options if you want to communicate online. Emails and text messages offer a more traditional approach of sending a message and then waiting for a reply. However, with constant access to the Internet and faster connections, instant messaging has become more popular. There are lots of services to choose from and the best thing to do is ask what your friends use and get the same one. Sometimes you have to pay for these but there are lots of fantastic free apps so you should choose one of those. When using these forms of communication, it is important to remember that they do not guarantee privacy and so you should be careful what you say and send, and you should be careful of using an appropriate tone for all of your messages.

## Texting and Instant Messaging

Generally, text and instant messaging is done between friends and people who know each other and so you should use the same sorts of language that you use in real life when you talk to those people. If the person is your friend then they probably understand your preferred way of communicating and so you can use this when texting. These messages are usually short and simple and many separate messages may be sent to complete a conversation. Some people use text speak and incorrect grammar, this is usually for convenience and to create an informal tone and is perfectly acceptable in text and instant messages. You should never use this language or grammar when you need to use a formal tone, such as messaging your boss about work. The best way to decide on the spelling and grammar is to mirror what the other person uses.

Some people use "kisses" at the end of their messages, these are shown by using the letter 'x'. The number of kisses implies the level of friendliness you want to use and sometimes you can use too many. Usually one kiss is friendly, two kisses is for good friends and three kisses is for someone you like romantically. However, the number of kisses used depends on the person and girls are more likely to use kisses than boys. The best way to work out how many kisses you use is to mirror the other person. If you are sending the first message and you haven't seen how many kisses the other person uses then you need to know if you are sending a friendly message or a straightforward practical message, if you are making arrangements to meet or to organise a school project then you probably don't need to use a kiss. Sometimes people may also use 'hugs' which look like an 'o', so if you see 'xoxo', this means kisses and hugs.

Sometimes you may need to send a text to someone that you don't know so well or that you know in a more formal way. For example, you may need to text an employer to tell them that you may be late for work if you have missed your train. In this case you should not use kisses as this is too friendly and you need to be more formal. It is best to apologise and stick to the facts, only including the relevant information. You can explain more about what happened when you see them in person.

You should try not to send too many messages to people because this can become annoying. The number of messages you should send depends on the person and what else they are doing at the time. You may send the first message but then you should wait for the other person to respond and only message them again when they have replied. Some people wait a few minutes before replying so that they don't look too keen. This makes it seem like you were not waiting for the person to message back, this suggests to the other person that you have other things to do at the time and makes you seem more busy and interesting, 3-5 minutes after they reply is fine for this. If you are genuinely busy then you should reply to the message when you have enough free time, or if you have a moment, reply to say that you will reply properly once you are free – this will let the person know that you have received the message and they should wait for you to get back to them. If the person has not replied after 1 hour then you can prompt them to reply, keeping your tone friendly. If they still do not reply then you should wait until the next day to text them again. If there is still no response then you should not message again. The person may just be busy but in that case they will get back to you when they have time, or they may not want to talk to you anymore.

Read Receipts are where the person sending a message to your smartphone can see that you've read their message, and what time you did this. It is usually best to turn these off. You can find out where to do this in your phone's guide or manual, but you'll probably find it in the "settings" menu under messaging.

Instant messaging apps like Whatsapp, Viber and Facebook Messenger, generally call for quicker responses than text messaging. The idea is to reply straight away and other people can see when you are online and so expect you to reply. However, if you are busy then you can set your status to offline or just not respond but be sure to explain that you were busy when you have time to reply to the other person. If the other person is the one not replying, then you should assume they are busy and give them plenty of time to reply. If they still have not replied the next day then you could send them a message to remind them to respond. Make sure your tone is friendly.

The flowchart on the next page can give you an idea of whether it is appropriate to send a message or not.

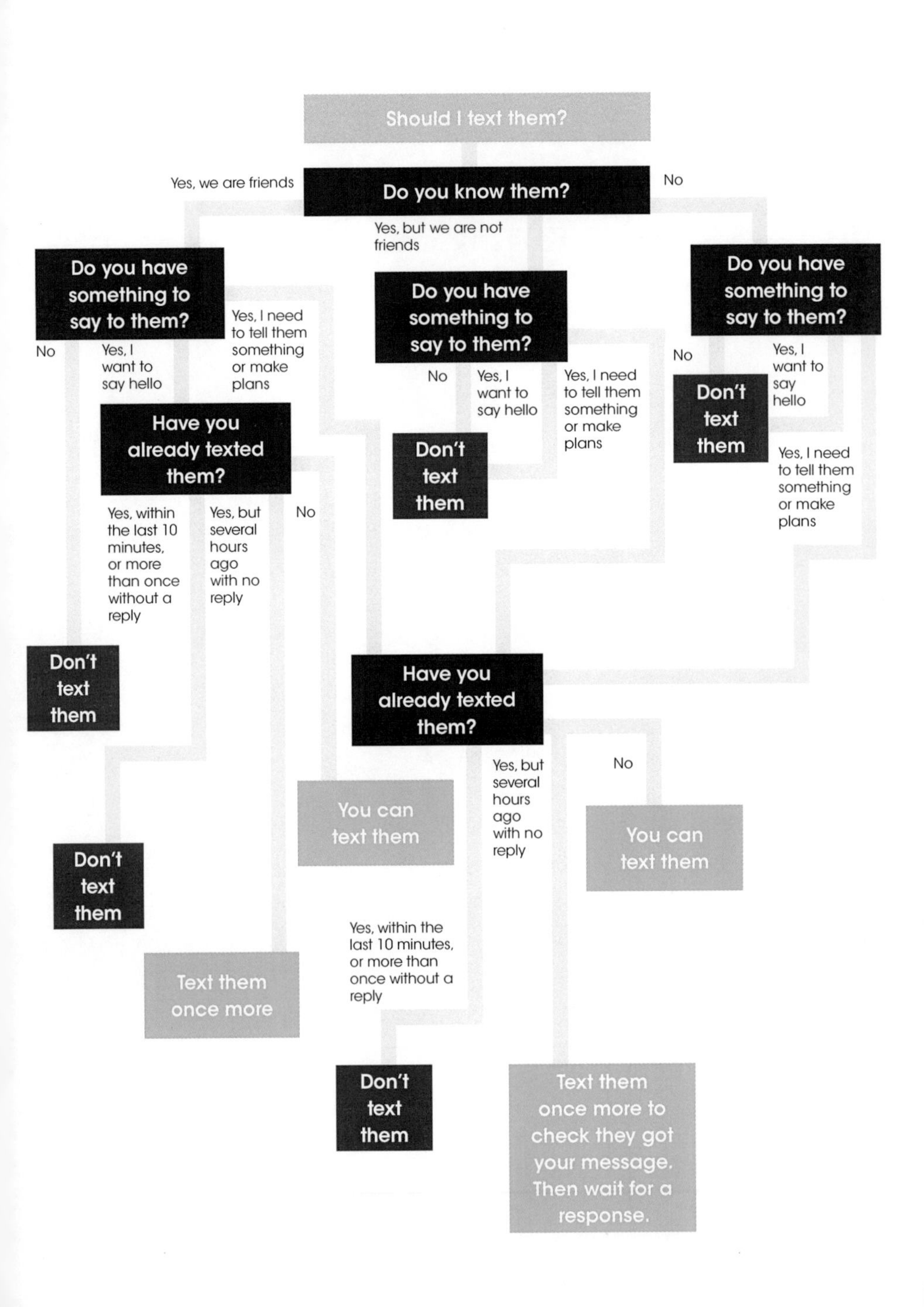
Should I text them?
Do you know them?
Yes, we are friends
Yes, but we are not friends
No
Do you have something to say to them?
No
Yes, I want to say hello
Yes, I need to tell them something or make plans
Have you already texted them?
Yes, within the last 10 minutes, or more than once without a reply
Yes, but several hours ago with no reply
No
Don't text them
Don't text them
You can text them
Text them once more
Do you have something to say to them?
No
Yes, I want to say hello
Yes, I need to tell them something or make plans
Don't text them
Do you have something to say to them?
No
Yes, I want to say hello
Yes, I need to tell them something or make plans
Don't text them
Have you already texted them?
Yes, but several hours ago with no reply
No
Yes, within the last 10 minutes, or more than once without a reply
You can text them
Don't text them
Text them once more to check they got your message. Then wait for a response.

### Facebook Messenger

Facebook Messenger is part of the main Facebook website and app, but also has its own app. You can use this to send instant messages to your Facebook friends as well as sending pictures and "stickers" which are sets of pictures you can download from Facebook. This is a way to send messages to groups of Facebook friends or individual Facebook friends and so it is a more private way to communicate. However, it is not totally private. People can take screenshots of anything you send and show them to other people so be very careful of what you send.

### Whatsapp

Whatsapp is an app that you can use on your phone to send messages, photos and video. You can have private and group chats and it uses your usual data plan or Wi-Fi so you don't have to pay for SMS messages. Remember though, this is not completely private; people can still save and screenshot what you send and then show it to others so be careful what you send.

**Snapchat**

Snapchat is a messaging app that allows you to send pictures and video. Videos will play through once and then disappear and you can choose how long you want pictures to appear for before they also disappear. You can set your privacy level to public or private; private means that you have to agree before someone can add you to their list of contacts.

This may seem like a very private way of sending pictures; especially ones that you don't want other people to see. However, people have found ways to 'grab' these pictures or take screenshots of them. This means that the pictures can still be seen after they are meant to have disappeared. The pictures can then be shared with other people who you may not know or who you do not want to see the pictures. You therefore need to think really carefully before you send someone a picture on Snapchat. Is it a picture that you are comfortable with other people seeing? If it isn't, then do not send it. If you do decide to send a picture, make sure that you only send it to a trusted friend. Never send a picture to somebody that you do not know.

Some people may try to get you to send them inappropriate pictures that you are not comfortable with taking. If anybody asks you to do this, it is important that you do not send him or her any pictures and that you tell a trusted relative immediately. They may also send you sexual pictures and this is also not acceptable so tell a trusted relative straight away.

Viber is an app that allows you to send messages, images and video as well as making phone calls all over the world, using your normal data plan or Wi-Fi. This means you do not have to pay any extra costs to use the app. Messages sent in this way can still be captured in a screenshot and shared with others so this is not a completely private way to communicate.

## Emails

Emails are usually used to communicate more information than text messages, or within a workplace environment. They are also a good way to receive information from companies and websites as well as to contact them directly. Emails can be a good way to message a friend you don't speak to often enough for text messages and so they can be very friendly in tone, but they are also used for more official functions and so you need to be aware of what tone you write them with. Emails give you the chance to put all of the relevant information in one message and then give the other person plenty of time to read your message and respond when they have time.

Generally speaking, people do not send another email to the same person until that person has replied. However, if you are contacting a business or company, you can send another email if they have not replied to you within two days. You need to be careful of your tone in emails because they are often sent to people who do not know you and they might not know your way of communicating or your sense of humour. Make sure you are always respectful and polite to the person you are emailing, read your email through before you send it. Because of the lack of body language for people to read, emails can come across much more harshly than you intend so try to make your emails very polite so that they are not misunderstood. You should also ensure that you have an appropriate email address to send emails from. You should not use anything that is suggestive, offensive, childish or political. It is best to use your name as your email address, using numbers and punctuation to make it unique. This ensures that you look professional to your colleagues or to companies and businesses that you are dealing with.

It is usually better to use proper language, grammar and punctuation in emails as this gives a more formal tone to the message and there is no word or character limit to make shortening words necessary. If you are emailing a friend then they may use abbreviations, in which case you can choose whether to use proper language or mirror their style. Emails allow you to write more and add more detail but you should only include what is important. Keep email messages to companies, businesses and colleagues short but effective, including only the information that will help the other person understand what you need. Sometimes a message that is very to the point in this way can come across as harsh to others so, if they are someone you know or work with, you can use emoticons (smiley faces, sad faces etc.) to soften the message. You should use these sparingly though and only with people you know. You can also choose an appropriate signing off phrase to show that you are not being harsh. "Kind regards" is a common phrase used to sign off emails, this tells the person that you expect them to take your email in a friendly way and that you wish them well. Some people also use "best wishes", both of these phrases are good because they are somewhere between formal and informal and so they can be used for almost all emails. If you are emailing to ask someone to do something for you though, you should sign off with a "Thank you" to show that you appreciate the person considering your request.

Sometimes people send nuisance emails to other people; these are known as 'spam'. These could be 'jokes' or emails telling you that something bad will happen if you don't send them on to other people. Do not forward these emails as many people find them annoying and some of them have viruses attached that may infect your computer and that of anyone you send it on to. These spam emails can also be messages claiming to have money that you could access if you give your bank details or telling you that you have won a big prize in a competition but you need to pay a customs fee to receive it. These are emails designed to take sensitive data from you or your money, delete them immediately if they enter your inbox. Most email providers have spam filters and a "Junk Mail" folder and you can sometimes change your settings to improve this protection. Never respond to these emails. Another kind of scam is called "phishing". This is when somebody sends you an email to try to get you to give him or her your usernames, passwords or bank details. They then use this information to access your accounts and use them; if it is your bank account then they can steal your money. The more sophisticated of these emails use fake websites that look like the real site for your bank and ask you to enter your details, to "confirm" them. This is always a scam, your bank will never contact you in this way and neither will any other site with which you have an account. If you receive something like this, it is best to contact the company with whom you have an account to tell them that someone is pretending to be them. Never respond to these emails or click on any links in the messages, and never give your personal details.

## Sexting

Some people choose to send pictures of their body to other people. If you are in a committed and loving relationship, and you are over 18, it is ok to send these kinds of pictures if you and your partner are both comfortable with doing this. However, relationships sometimes break down, and there are examples of people posting sexually explicit photos of former partners on the internet in order to embarrass them. So it's best to be cautious.

You should never send nude or sexually explicit photos to your partner unless he/she has asked for them, because you may scare them or make them feel uncomfortable. Even if you've been asked to send them, it's your choice to send them or not, and, as we said, you should be cautious. Some people think that it is funny to share these pictures with other people who are not meant to see them. They might do this to embarrass you or to make fun of you. You should never send these types of picture to anyone that you would not show your body to in person, and even then you should seriously think about the possible consequences before sending them. If you have just started going out with someone then do not send pictures because they may be taking advantage of you or they could be lying about being your boyfriend or girlfriend to get pictures or video, either because they want to look at them or because they want to embarrass you by showing them to other people.

In the UK, it is illegal to take or send or be in possession of sexual images of people under the age of 18. This can include photographs, videos, or even tracings of sexually explicit photographs. Breaking any of these rules is a criminal offence and you could go to prison. And it's not just sexually explicit images: the law covers "indecent" images as well – and that would certainly include some nude photographs. If you are under 18 then anyone asking you to send indecent or sexual pictures or video

to them is committing a crime and you must tell a trusted relative and not send the pictures or video. You should never ask for these types of pictures from someone who is under 18 years old, and you should not send any of these types of picture to someone who is under 18. If you do, you will be committing a crime and may get in serious trouble.
It is also illegal for anyone in a position of power over you to have sexually explicit images of you because this is considered to be an abuse of that power. This includes parents, teachers and any other professionals you work with. If anybody asks you for this sort of image then you should tell a relative that you trust.

Another form of sexting is when people simulate sex with each other through written messages. This is sometimes called "cyber sex", "cybering" or "text sex". People do this to excite themselves and usually they also want to excite the other person. Sometimes people do this together and masturbate. This is something that you may want to do with a loving and committed partner, if you are over 16. However, engaging in this activity with somebody under 16 is illegal and you should be extremely careful.

It is important to be aware that some people try to take advantage of vulnerable adults, and persuade them to engage in cybersex, for their own pleasure or amusement. You should never take part in this type of communication with anyone that you don't know, and if someone you don't know sends you any messages like this, you should ignore them and tell somebody you trust. Sometimes people will start this kind of conversation with you so that they can show the conversation to other people because they think it is funny to upset and embarrass you. This means you should be very careful of who you send these messages to and be sure that they won't show other people. If in doubt, don't send.

## Video Calls

Video calls are like telephone calls except that you can see the other person you are talking to. This means that you can talk to people all over the world, in real time, and see them at the same time. You can do this on your computer using a webcam or you can use your phone with various apps. If you use your phone, the call will be made with the built-in camera in your phone. Skype is the most popular video-calling programme for desktop computers and laptops but there are plenty of other programmes that offer similar features. You can also download a Skype app and use this on your phone. iPhones also have a very popular app called Facetime, which allows you to video call anyone with an iPhone for free, as long as you have a Wi-Fi connection.

Sometimes people may use message boards and other websites to meet people and then arrange to speak to them via a video call. A lot of the time this is perfectly reasonable and can be a great way to make new friends that share your interests. However, nasty people who want to get to know you better so that they can take advantage of you can also use this. This means that, if you want to talk to someone via video call, you should tell a relative you trust and ask him or her to help you to set it up. The relative can stay with you while you talk, until you feel comfortable and the relative is happy that the person is appropriate for you to speak to. If the conversation begins to make you feel uncomfortable in any way, including becoming aggressive, confusing or sexually explicit, you should hang up immediately. Tell the relative what happened and ask them for help. This will keep you safe and prevent people from being able to take advantage of you.

**Facetime**

Facetime is an app you can use on Apple devices to make video calls to other Apple devices. You need to know the person's phone number and have a Wi-Fi connection.

**Skype**

Skype is a programme that you can install onto your computer or phone. It allows you to make phone calls and video calls over the Internet for free. It also has an instant messaging function where you can send messages, files and images to other people. You create a contact list of people you might talk to. These should only be people you know in real life. If you meet someone online and you would like to chat to them more and see them in the video call then you should tell a trusted relative you want to do this and ask them to help you to set it up. The relative can stay until you are comfortable being left to talk with the other person. This can help to ensure that you do not end up talking to someone who is inappropriate.

# Forums and Chatrooms

Forums and chatrooms offer a different way to communicate with other people and are usually based around a particular interest or topic. This can mean that they are a great place to meet new people as you already know that you have a shared interest.

## Forums

A forum is a website or app that has different topics or 'discussions' that you can join and type in messages and comments or answers to questions. Other users also post and then you can start to have a group conversation. All other users of the forum can see the messages; message board or 'board' and they can join in the conversation too. Forums are often organised around a particular subject or fandom of a certain thing but they usually also have more general chat 'threads' or topics. Forums can be based around all sorts of things but some examples are games, football teams, musical artists or even things like mental health.

The term 'lurker' is used to describe people who go onto forums but do not post anything. They just read the comments of others. Sometimes these people sign up to the site but other times they don't have a screen name or account and just visit the site to read other people's posts. This is generally not a problem but can be frowned upon because the idea of these sites is to contribute to the community.

**Wrong Planet**

Wrong Planet is a forum designed specifically for people with autism and other neurological differences. It has discussion forums as well as chat rooms for real time conversations, regular articles and how-to guides.

## Chat rooms

Chat rooms are websites that allow you to join different groups or 'rooms' to talk to other people in real time. They are a lot like instant messaging but with different people, many of whom you will not know. You can arrange to meet friends and some chat rooms allow you to make your own private rooms to allow you to just talk to your friends. Some chat rooms are based around a specific shared interest or to discuss particular topics and others are more general or offer lots of different 'rooms' or groups.

Some chat rooms, like Habbo Hotel and Club Penguin, are specifically designed to be used by young people and children. These usually have more games and activities to play and do alongside the chat room aspect of the sites. They also have moderators and report functions in case anything happens that you are not comfortable with.

Because you can talk to total strangers using a screen name or an avatar, chat rooms can be quite dangerous. They can be used by nasty people to meet vulnerable adults and young people, because it is easy to hide their identity, for example, a much older man could pretend to be a young girl so that he can make friends with a young girl on a chat room. These people may deliberately seek out young and vulnerable people to engage in sexual activities with them, for their own pleasure. If you are under 16 then these people are called paedophiles but if you are over 16 they can still be very scary and unpleasant people. They usually get worse over time as they build a relationship with you; this is called 'grooming'. They use their communication with you to get to know you. They may pretend to be your friend at first and make you feel good and feel that you should do nice things for them to make them happy. But then they may start to ask you to show them pictures of your body or talk to them in a sexually explicit way. Sometimes they may then become nasty and tell you that unless you carry on then they will tell people about the pictures that you have sent or show them to other people, this is called 'extortion'. They may also ask you to meet them for sex. If anything like this happens or you are uncomfortable in any way with anything that happens online, you must tell a trusted relative straight away so that they can help you.

Meeting somebody you have met on the Internet can be incredibly dangerous and some people are very nasty and potentially extremely violent. You should never meet anyone that you have met online, on your own. If you think you have made a good friend then you should meet them in a busy public place and take a trusted relative with you. It is very easy for them to seem very nice and kind when they only communicate through messages and video calls because they can lie quite easily and there are no visual cues to help you work out if they are telling the truth.

**Habbo Hotel**

Habbo Hotel is a chat room designed for teenagers and young adults. It is set up to look like a hotel, playing on the idea of chat 'rooms', it has various rooms associated with a hotel, such as a lobby and pool area. It also has private rooms that users can build, decorate and furnish themselves. The chat is general in all rooms and users can explore freely and talk to new people. Users also design an avatar choosing their hair and clothes.

Habbo Hotel is mostly used by young teenagers to meet up with members of the opposite sex and is sometimes used for virtual dates and relationships.

**Club Penguin**

Club Penguin is owned by Disney and allows users to create a penguin and then play games, explore the world and meet new friends. The sign up asks for a parent's email address and then the parent signs up on the child's behalf and this gives them the chance to choose between safe chat mode which is filtered and super safe mode which means the child can only choose from selected phrases and can only see messages made in super safe mode by other users. Children with access to an email address could sign up themselves, but the chat function is reasonably safe.

# Gaming and Internet Subcultures

## Online Gaming

There is a whole host of games that can be played online. Some games, like Minecraft and World of Warcraft, are purchased and then played online on a variety of different servers with different settings and standards for gameplay. Other games are one-player games for PC and consoles but also have online and multiplayer modes that allow you to work with other players or play against them. Sometimes the games will automatically assign teams for you to play on and others require you to find and build alliances and allegiances to create your own teams. All of these games have online chat functions to allow you to speak to other gamers and some have associated message boards that allow you to talk about the game and potentially meet new people. Acronyms are used frequently and leet speak originated with gamers and so you will see this used a lot. There are also different acronyms and words that are used differently in each game. If you see a word or acronym you don't understand, you can always look it up online or ask the person what they mean.

Microtransactions are another term for "in-game purchases". In many games, the player will have the opportunity to obtain virtual equipment, clothing, or access special areas or content by making a payment. Remember, these are real purchases made with real money and can add up over time to be extremely expensive. Be very careful what you buy within games. If it is not your credit or debit card, make sure you have permission from whoever owns the card.

## Internet Subculture

The term 'subculture' refers to things that are popular but not with the mainstream. There are lots of websites that regular users of the Internet will be familiar with, but that may not be used regularly by more casual users of the Internet who tend to be limited to mainstream social media, games and lifestyle apps.

These sites create and maintain running jokes and use different language and acronyms to communicate, creating a sense of community as well as exclusion of all those not "in the know". They also bring together people based on specific interests such as art and other creative pursuits or different interests in music and fashion. If you have a particular passion then you are likely to be able to find a website dedicated to it and meet other likeminded people.

## Memes

Memes are ideas or styles that pass amongst people quickly and effectively. These are sometimes images or words; they can also be gifs or videos. These are often described as having "gone viral" which just means that they have spread very quickly. This comes from the fact that viruses spread between people very quickly and are highly contagious. However, viral memes are not harmful and they are not a form of computer virus, they are just fun items that spread quickly.

Lolcats are a popular style of meme. They are pictures of cats with captions written on them. They use poor spelling and grammar to suggest what the cat might be saying in the image, because cats do not have a good understanding of proper English.

This same style of an image with a text caption written over it is very common and there is a huge array of different kinds. Each image is usually associated with a specific joke and people come up with new versions. For example, 'doge' consists of Shiba Inu dogs and text written in comic sans font, sometimes in a variety of colours. The text is broken English phrases around the picture, often using the word 'wow' as well as phrases using 'such', 'much', 'so', 'many' and 'very'. People then started writing messages to each other in this form too.

## Acronyms

Acronyms are short sets of letters that people use to communicate a longer sentence or idea. They are used to simplify language and make more efficient use of time and space in a message. They are also used by young people to make it more difficult for other people (mostly adults) to understand what is being said. There is another set of acronyms and words made up of different combinations of letters, numbers and symbols, which form a kind of code. This is called "leet speak" and is designed to exclude people who do not understand the language, and create a sense of community for those that do. "Leet" comes from the word 'elite' and is usually written in numbers as '1337'.

| What they say | What they mean |
|---|---|
| asl/'a/s/l' | Age, sex, location: asking for your details |
| wtf | What the f*** |
| wth | What the hell |
| omg | Oh my god |
| omfg | Oh my f***ing god |
| zomg | Oh my god (sarcastic) |
| lol / lolz | Laughing out loud |
| lmao | Laughing my a*s off |

| | |
|---|---|
| rofl | Rolling on the floor laughing |
| gtfo | Get the f*** out |
| afk | Away from keyboard |
| brb | Be right back |
| stfu | Shut the f*** up |
| b4 | Before |
| h8 | Hate |
| gr8 | Great |
| iirc | If I remember correctly |
| idk | I don't know |
| 2day | Today |
| atm | At the moment |
| bf/gf | Boyfriend/girlfriend |
| dm/pm | Direct message/ Private message |
| ftw | For the win (that is good) |
| nvm / nm | Never mind |
| nsfw | Not safe for work (graphic or sexually explicit) |
| fb | Facebook |
| imo/imho | In my opinion/in my humble opinion |
| fyi | For your information |
| ikr | I know, right? |
| irl | In real life |
| k/kk | OK |
| fml | f *** my life (my life sucks) |
| o rly | Oh really? (sometimes sarcastic) |
| np | No problem |
| ppl | People |
| RT | Retweet (on Twitter) |
| srsly | Seriously |
| tl;dr | Too long; didn't read |
| btw | By the way |
| ur | you are, you're or your |
| tmi | Too much information |

### Vine

Vine is a website where users create short videos that then play on a loop. They can share these online, and search for and view videos made by others. They can also be shared to other social networking sites.

### Gifs

Gifs are animations made up of pictures that are shown very quickly so that they look like a film. They can be posted just like pictures online but they move. People can make these from videos using a converter or they can make animated ones from scratch. These can be shared anywhere online and saved on your computer.

### Imgur

Imgur (pronounced image-er) is an image sharing website. Users can upload photos and pictures and they are visible by others. They can be commented on and rated as good or bad. Imgur creates a unique page for each photo so it allows you to link to that picture to share it with others.

### Buzzfeed

Buzzfeed is a website that posts news and comment about current affairs. They also create fun and silly quizzes and give updates on new memes and popular topics as well as producing lists of facts and images that are amusing.

### DeviantArt

DeviantArt is a website that allows users to post artwork of all kinds and share it with other users. You can add drawings, writing and digital art, or anything else you have created. People can then comment on it, saying what they like and dislike and hopefully offering some constructive criticism if necessary. Because of this, it is possible that you may receive negative comments and opinions and this can be upsetting. However, if someone is making a genuine suggestion about your work then it may well be because they are being supportive and suggesting ways you could become a better artist. DevMeets are organised for people who use DeviantArt to meet up and socialise. These take place all over the country on different dates and you can find out more about them on the website.

### Fan Fiction

Fan art is art drawn of characters from a pre-existing story but they are often changed or altered in some way or placed in a situation not relevant to the original story. For example, there are gender-swapped versions of Disney characters and characters from The Simpsons drawn to look like humans.

Fan fiction is writing that uses characters from pre-existing stories. This writing sometimes continues the story after it finished in the original version. Sometimes it uses the characters but puts them in an entirely new situation or with characters from a different story. Other examples use the characters and general world from the original story but alter key parts to create a new narrative. Fan fiction often has a romantic or sexual element in which key characters are involved in relationships. This can be with characters from their own story or 'crossover' relationships with characters from other stories.

## Avatars/Screen names

Some websites need each user to have a unique name to make sure that it is clear who is talking in a discussion and who is responsible for what content. This is why some websites ask you to make a username or screen name when you sign up. This is sometimes to ensure you have anonymity. You then use that name while you are using that website or forum. A lot of people try to use the same screen name across sites so that they can be recognised by other people who use the same websites. But this is not always possible because someone may already have that name on the other sites.

Avatars are characters that are used to represent the user. Sometimes these are small pictures or animations that appear alongside posts and sometimes these are more like video game characters. Some chat rooms such as Habbo Hotel and Club Penguin use animated characters as avatars for users. Some websites and apps also allow users to design their own avatar so it looks either like them or how they want it to look.

## Griefing

Griefing is when a player uses game features in a way that deliberately harasses and upsets other gamers. The purpose of griefing is generally just to annoy other players and happens more often in online games. Minecraft is vulnerable to griefing because other players can steal and destroy your items and buildings. This can be very frustrating and upsetting. You can usually report this to the admins on the server. However, some people think that this kind of griefing adds to the variety in the game and so do not do anything to stop it. If you are worried about this then there are servers that limit or ban completely this kind of activity. AutCraft is an autism-specific server that monitors bad language and nasty comments as well as all forms of griefing. You can build your own server and adjust the settings to suit what you want. Bukkit is a website for plugins for Minecraft servers which help you to control various aspects of your server.

Massively Multiplayer Online Role Playing Games (MMORPGs) have different rules on different servers and in different modes. In World of Warcraft, griefing is considered acceptable behaviour only if there is a way for the target to remedy to situation in player vs. player (PvP) mode, such as getting together a group to overwhelm the griever. However some people grief people in their own faction or without their PvP flag up, which means that the griefing cannot be counteracted. If this is the case then the behaviour can be reported to the gamemaster. Some games red flag someone who has been reported for griefing, until the gamemaster deals with them, to let people know that they have previously been reported. There have also been software changes added to some games to address the most common types of griefing behaviour as well as separate servers for people who do not want to be vulnerable to attack.

It is important that you do not grief other people, as it is annoying and could be upsetting for them. It can ruin their chance of enjoying the game and is unfair on them. A lot of online games give you the chance to work co-operatively and you should try to do this with players who are doing well, then they may be able to help you to get more items and information about the game. If someone else grieves you, then you should report it – how to do this will vary depending on the game. It is also important that you research different servers and their rules so that you can make an informed choice about which one to use.

Some people do silly things during a game. They may cause their avatars to run into things or deliberately end their life and "respawn". It's best to try not to get annoyed by this sort of behaviour and ignore it if you can.

### World of Warcraft

World of Warcraft (WoW) is a Massively Multiplayer Online Role Playing Game (MMORPG) in which players create characters and use them as avatars to complete quests and raids and explore different worlds and adventures. Players can work together as teams and chat to each other in game. You can also collect items and weapons to improve your characters.

### Minecraft

Minecraft is a game in which users can mine, collect and craft with different minerals. They can combine different minerals and items to create new objects, weapons and clothes. They can also build structures such as houses, castles and palaces. Games are hosted on servers and different servers have different rules and numbers of other players using them. There are animals that players can use to get more items and other creatures that will attack the player, but these can be fought or hidden from. You can also use the chat function to talk to other players, work together in teams or give gifts to friends.

### Bukkit

Bukkit is a website that provides various add-ons for Minecraft servers. This means you can make your own server and customise it to work exactly how you want it to. This can include removing the possibility of stealing or destroying properties and changing the way the chat function works as well as who can join the server. This is a good way to protect your enjoyment of the game, ensuring that your character is not vulnerable to griefing or inappropriate chat content.

## Trolling/Flaming

Trolling is when people on a website say things with the deliberate intention of annoying others and provoking a response, this can include attempting to interrupt or disrupt a conversation or group by changing the subject. Flaming is linked to this and the two often overlap, however, flaming is generally considered to be angry or nasty comments to insult other users. The main difference is that a 'flamer' posts insulting things because they are angry and want to express that, whereas a 'troll' posts insulting things with the main intention of provoking a reaction. Sometimes people want both of these things and the two things overlap. Attention is the main reason for people to troll or flame. Flamers generally want to vent their emotions and feelings and get a reaction for that, whereas trolls will generally seek any kind of attention. Trolls like to feel that they are powerful and have disrupted a conversation or group and upset and annoyed the other users. This is an immature thing to do. It makes the experience of website users less enjoyable and can become very serious when it targets vulnerable people. Trolls will sometimes post offensive comments on memorial pages for people who have died or on very serious news stories.

The phrase "don't feed the trolls" (DFTT) means that, because trolls are only looking for attention and want to provoke a reaction, the best thing to do is to ignore them. If they do not get the reaction they want then they will generally go away. This can be difficult to do if you do not recognise that they are just 'trolling' and they have said something you find offensive. But if you see something that upsets you, you can usually report it to a moderator or gamemaster or admin for the site. Do not allow yourself to be upset by offensive things you see online. Often the poster doesn't even believe what they say, they just think it is fun to provoke others.

Some people troll in teams and groups to increase their effectiveness in causing distress for others. It is possible that someone could approach you to join his or her group. You should not join in with this behaviour because you may really upset someone. However, you may also get into trouble for trolling without meaning to. When posting online, you should be careful not to write comments when you are angry or upset because this may mean that you write something that isn't very nice or kind. You should also be careful to only write things that add something useful to the conversation that people are already having. If you want to discuss something else then it may be better to find another thread if you are on a forum, or another group.

Some websites hide comments that have been reported or have been marked down as unpopular and this helps you to avoid comments posted by trolls. Other sites have a 'thumbs up' and 'thumbs down' rating system and you can choose not to see comments that have received a lot of thumbs down ratings. You can report comments you find upsetting and offensive but you should generally not respond to a troll or a flamer, because that is exactly what they want you to do.

**Moderators/Gamemasters/Admins**

Moderators, gamemasters and admins are all names for people who look after forums, game servers and websites. These are people who have some control and powers to help you if you encounter difficulties or anything inappropriate on any site, game or forum. You can report anything that worries or upsets you to these people and they will try to help you and deal with any other user that is involved.

## In-Game Chat

Chatting in games is generally supposed to support players to work together within the game. This can help them to share information and advice as well as co-operating to complete adventures, quests and projects. However, sometimes people have more general conversations using the in-game chat function. If you know a player in real life or you have played the game with them before, then it is usually ok to have general discussion, but if you don't know the player, it is best to limit your conversation to game-related topics.

It is important that you stop talking to someone if they ask you to or if they move their character away from yours. If you have tried to speak to them and they are active in the game but do not reply after 10 minutes then they may not want to talk to you anymore and you should leave them alone. It is possible that they are busy or distracted but in this case you should wait for them to come to you to say that they are ready to talk again. Do not send anyone the same messages more than twice and do not keep messaging someone who does not want to talk to you because this is harassment and you may upset the other person and possibly get in trouble with a gamemaster or admin. Equally, if anyone is harassing you and will not stop talking to you or leave you alone, you should report them to a gamemaster or admin.

Other types of messages that are inappropriate are anything that is sexually explicit or violent in any way. You should also avoid anything that is gory, such as describing injuries in detail, or anything offensive or hateful. Some hate speech is considered a crime and so you could get in a lot of trouble but there are also things that are very offensive and might upset other people. Do not attack people for their gender, race or religion as this could make people feel excluded from the game. It is not nice to make any kind of personal attack or insult another player and you shouldn't do this. If anyone sends you a message like this then you should report him or her immediately to the gamemaster or admin. Swearing is not always against the rules for messaging but it can make your messages sound very aggressive and unpleasant so you should avoid it. You can disable text communication in most games if you choose to, but it's better to wait for an appropriate moment to do this if you can. This could be at the end of a conversation, level, mission or game.

Many people use headsets to communicate verbally with other players in a game. Some players will not respond well to people who do not use headsets as they think they are ignoring them or being rude. Some people with autism may struggle to communicate verbally and concentrate on the game at the same time. If this is the case for you, it can be helpful to use the headset to listen and follow instructions, but tell your team mates that you won't talk much as you find it easier to concentrate on the game that way.

## Staying Safe Online

Being connected to other people, via the Internet, can be a fantastic thing and allow great communication of ideas and information. However, there are some very nasty people in the world and they can go online as well. This means that you have to be very careful to protect yourself and your data and always be careful that you behave sensibly. You should keep all passwords safe and secret and you should be aware that it is easier for people to lie if you have not met them in real life.

DO...

- Make sure anti-virus and anti-spyware programmes are running at all times and make sure they are up to date.
- Always have strong anti-spam and anti-phishing tools installed on

your computer and set them to update automatically.

- REMEMBER: when you post anything online, it is there forever. There is no way to get it back. Therefore, you need to think very carefully before you post something.

- Ask a responsible and trusted relative if you are unsure about anything on the Internet. This is especially important when you are spending money online – you need to make sure you are only paying the correct amount to a trusted site.

- Reply to people's posts on your wall or messages they send you. It is very easy for people to see on social networking sites if you are ignoring them. However, not everybody checks their text messages or social networking sites constantly, so they may not reply immediately. If someone takes a while to get back to you, they may be busy and unable to respond straight away.

- If you only want to send a message to one person or a small group of people, texting or using the personal messaging functions on social networking sites are the best ways to do this. Both Twitter and Facebook allow you to use this system.

- Make sure to check if a friend is ok with you posting something that involves them. This may be a photo, a tweet, a status update, or a comment. They may not want something about them to be made public, so always ask for permission before uploading something related to your friends. If they ask you to delete or remove something that you have previously posted, always do so as soon as you can.

- Remember that general social skills that you may have learnt or developed still apply to online situations and conversations. It is still rude to make critical comments about someone online, and it is still nice to ask people questions about themselves and what they have been doing recently. Only ask people questions that you wouldn't feel awkward or anxious answering yourself, and remember that while some things may be true, they may not be good things to say to someone (for example, comments about their appearance). This is particularly relevant on social media sites, where you can write comments about people's photos. Don't post negative or hurtful remarks about a photo that somebody posts of himself or herself online.

- Social media and texting are not a replacement for meeting your friends and family. Whilst it may be easier to contact people on the Internet or mobile phones, face-to-face meetings are still most people's favourite way of talking to each other. Try and arrange to meet your friends regularly so you can keep in contact and to practise your social skills.

## DON'T...

- Don't give anyone – even your best friend – your password for your computer or website profiles. Always check to see if anyone is around before you enter a password.

- Avoid using an inappropriate screen or domain name. Don't use a screen name that gives away information about your age, or where you live, such as JohnSWalsall17@hotmail.co.uk

- Don't share information with a friend of a friend. Even though your friend might know them, they are not necessarily your friend too.

- Avoid forwarding chain emails. They are likely to be scams and may harm your computer or the computer of people you send them to.

- Do not be fooled by spam emails. They are tricks designed to get you to buy something you might not really want or enter your personal data so it can be stolen.

- Do not post when you are angry, anxious, or stressed, as you may post something you later regret. Take some time out away from you computer, laptop, or phone before deciding whether or not you want to post something.

- Don't post anything that could later be used against you. Make sure that any status or photo you upload will not cause you any embarrassment later on. A good rule to use is to avoid putting anything online that you wouldn't want your close family or future boss to see.

- Don't be a social media addict. It may be tempting to constantly talk to your friends online and post content for others to see, but too much time spent on the Internet can have a negative impact on other areas of your life. Similarly, constant posting, updating, and uploading can cause other people to ignore what you say online.

## Privacy

Sometimes it is difficult to know what is and what isn't private online. As lots of sites – and your mobile phone – let you talk directly to a person, it might make you think that everything that you are saying and doing is private. However, it is important to remember that this is not always true and that a lot of the time, something that you think is private may actually be seen by lots of people. There are some important rules for some sites that you need to think about to help you protect your privacy.

## Cyber Stalking

Cyber stalking is just like normal stalking and can be annoying or potentially scary and threatening. If you are worried that it is happening to you, tell a trusted relative immediately. You should also be aware that, if someone thinks you are behaving like a cyber stalker then they may feel annoyed or frightened and you should stop. Stalking means you make contact with someone on a regular basis, who does not want you to make contact with them. A stalker can be anyone, a stranger or someone you know, and they can have a range of reasons for doing it. Stalking is a criminal offence in the UK and so you should be careful that you do not behave in this way or report it immediately, to a trusted relative, if you think it is happening to you.

The difference between stalking and cyber stalking is that 'cyber' means it is online as opposed to physically stalking you by following you or visiting you house. Cyber stalkers often target accounts including bank accounts and social media accounts. They do this to access and steal your money and may use your social media pages to post on your behalf. They may post things that make you look bad or contact your friends and family. They may also track what you are doing and where you will be using the information you post online and harass you using different communication methods on the Internet. There is also a small possibility that they could use this information to find you in real life. This can be scary and dangerous and if you have any concerns make sure you tell a trusted relative what is going on.

## Webcams

Webcams are cameras that connect to your computer. You can use these to take pictures and video as well as to make video calls using the Internet. Sometimes these are bought separately to your computer and just plug in when you want to use them; other webcams are built into the computer itself. These look like a small lens at the top of the screen and usually have a little hole and a light next to them. The hole is the microphone and the light should tell you when the camera is on.

Other people using certain kinds of hacking software can access Webcams remotely. This means that they can turn on your webcam without you knowing and watch you using your computer or even take pictures of recordings to keep for themselves. They can also use this method to watch you type in passwords to gain access to your accounts. You should always unplug your webcam if it is not built into the computer, or cover the lens with a small piece of paper if it is a built-in camera. This is extremely rare and unlikely to happen to you so it is not something that you should worry about, but it is a good idea to ensure that you keep yourself and your details safe by removing or covering your camera when you are not using it.

## Bullying

Bullying is a common occurrence throughout society. It is very upsetting and unpleasant and the Internet has now made it possible to bully people 24/7. If you experience bullying, the most important thing is to tell a relative that you trust and ask them to help and advise you. Private messaging services can be used to harass people and to encourage them to send pictures or videos of embarrassing things, which are then passed on. There have been several cases of bad pictures and videos being sent around to hundreds of people to embarrass and shame individual people. Some people have even killed themselves because the bullying was so severe and so relentless.

This can be scary to think about but what is important to remember is that if you are bullied, you are not alone. Other people have been through it to and lots of people really care about you and how you are feeling. Do not respond to bullies, their aim is to provoke you to respond and to feel like they have some power over you. It is also vital that you tell a trusted relative as soon as the bullying begins.

Some sites offer their users anonymity including sites like Whisper and

Ask.fm and this allows people to post things without getting in trouble for that. It is important to keep yourself safe and be careful whom you share things with. You can also avoid these anonymous sites; this will mean that people cannot bully you in this way. It is also very important to remember that you should not bully other people. Even if other people are being nasty or spiteful to someone, and even if they are your friends, you should not bully anyone. If you don't like someone then you do not have to spend time with them but you should not send them nasty messages or join in with others to be cruel to them.

**Ask.fm**

Ask.fm is a site that allows users to sign up anonymously and post questions to have them answered by others. The site has become infamous for stories of bullying and has been linked to several suicides. There is no report feature and so there is no protection if you find anything on the site upsetting or inappropriate. We recommend that you do not use this site or the associated app.

**Whisper**

Whisper is a website and app that allows users to sign up anonymously and type secrets to post online. Users choose a photo to display along with their secret, they can select this from a range provided by Whisper, or they can add their own. Other users then comment on the secrets. The Whisper website and app both collect identifying information from users so you are only anonymous to other users, not to the website. The site has been used to bully people, as some users have posted secrets or nasty comments about a person displayed over unflattering or unpleasant pictures. The site is moderated and you can report any content that you think is upsetting or inappropriate. We recommend that you do not use this site or the associated app.

# Summary

We hope you have enjoyed this book and that you have learnt some new and interesting things about the Internet and social networks. You can keep this book somewhere safe so that you can refer to it if you need to in the future. You can use the next few pages to make notes about what you've learnt.

The Internet is always changing and adapting as people invent new ways to communicate. This means that some of the information in this book may not always be 100% up to date. However, the principles you've learnt, like mirroring, and tone will be the same, even if the communication tools change.

# Notes

# Notes

# Notes